# Shelley Rotner

# Senses at the Seashore

M Millbrook Press    Minneapolis

To my parents and our shared love of the ocean—S. R.

Millbrook Press
A division of Lerner Publishing Group, Inc.
241 First Avenue North
Minneapolis, Minnesota 55401 U.S.A.

Website address: www.lernerbooks.com

Rotner, Shelley.
Senses at the seashore / Shelley Rotner.
p. cm.
Summary: A child shares the sights, sounds, smells, touches, and tastes of a day at the seashore.
ISBN-13: 978-0-7613-2897-1 (lib. bdg. : alk. paper)
ISBN-10: 0-7613-2897-1 (lib. bdg. : alk. paper)
[1. Seashore—Fiction.   2. Senses and sensation—Fiction.]   I. Title.
PZ7.R752Se 2006
[E]—dc22                                      2005006151

Manufactured in the United States of America
4 - DP - 12/1/12

At the seashore . . .

# See
**the blue water.**

**Hear**
the waves
crash.

# Smell
## the
## lotion.

**Touch** the cold water.

**Taste** the salty seawater.

**See** a fishing boat go by.

Smell
the fresh fish.

# Touch
the warm
sand.

**Hear** the seashell.

**Taste**
your yummy
sandwich.

**Smell** the roses in bloom.

# Hear the gulls cry.

# Touch
## a soft feather.

**See** the fluffy white clouds.

# Taste
a fruity
pop.

**See** a kite flying high.

**Smell**
the seaweed
at low tide.

**Touch** its slippery surface.

# Hear
### the lifeguard's whistle.

# Taste
## the sweet juicy watermelon.

**Hear**
your
parents
call.

**Smell**
the bonfire.

**Touch** the fluffy towel.

**Taste**
your delicious dinner.

**See** the sunset.

At the seashore, there's so much to
**see, hear, smell, taste, touch.**